Why Do Metals Rust?

An Easy Read Chemistry Book for Kids

Children's Chemistry Books

BABY PROFESSOR

EDUCATION KIDS

Speedy Publishing LLC
40 E. Main St. #1156
Newark, DE 19711
www.speedypublishing.com

Have you ever noticed the reddish-brown flakes on metal? This is called rust. As iron is subjected to oxygen it creates a new substance known as iron oxide. This happens only when the level of oxygen is present enough to react. This is considered a chemical reaction. Iron will never react with oxygen in the air since it moves in a combined state with the other oxygen and at this point the oxygen is not able to react. So then why does the iron rust?

The oxygen that is present in the air and dissolves with water becomes separated from other oxygen and proceeds to move its own way. Thus, it does not remain in a combined state. The iron can now react with the singular state of oxygen, and we can agree that metal becomes rusted only when moisture, iron, and oxygen react together. The brown flakes, known as hydrated ferric oxide, is what we know as rust. Rust will weaken the metal enough that it can be broken easily.

ELASTIC ADHESIVE
EMERGENCY DRESSINGS

When salts are added, the reaction speeds up. The iron oxide is bulky and porous and allows the oxygen and iron to react further causing additional oxidation. If this is not stopped at this point, then the metal changes to ferric oxide, also known as rust, and becomes weak enough that it breaks easily. This can be prevented by not allowing the mixture of water and oxygen to come into contact with the iron or by coating it with paints, oil, grease, or something similar. If this coating is removed the iron will proceed to rust.

The movement of electrons from one substance to another substance is known as corrosion. Redox reactions occur when salt is present in the water and improves the ability of the water to move the electrons.

Oxidation

Oxidation occurs when something loses electrons, gains atoms or oxygen atoms and loses hydrogen atoms.

Reduction

Reduction is the opposite of Oxidation.

When both of these occur it is known as a redux reaction.

The rusting that occurs in metals is oxidation of the metal to the metal oxide. Water then acts as a medium and transfers the electrons and the salt which speeds up the corrosion process. This is considered an electrochemical process when iron loses its electrons from oxidation resulting in the water breaking into the hydroxide ions and oxygen.

The iron then has oxidized reactions with the hydroxide ions and oxygen and forms metal oxide. The salts then remain even when the water is no longer present and again start rusting when they again come in contact with moisture. This is why metals become rusted quicker if they are near beaches or salty locations.

Iron oxidation occurs in a reaction requiring three components: an anode, a cathode, and an electrolyte. An atom releasing an electron during a reaction is called an anode. Another atom taking the electron is known as the cathode. The medium by which the electron travels are known as the electrolyte. Being highly conductive, Iron can be its anode and cathode. Carbonic acid is often the electrolyte.

Carbonic acid forms once a drop a water, more than likely rain, drops through air and then takes some carbon dioxide. The carbon dioxide then mixes with water's molecule and results in a slightly acidic compound that can rapidly degrade any anode it hits. On iron's surface, carbonic acid allows the electron flow from various iron atoms, acting as anodes, to other of the iron's atoms which act as cathodes. This quickly results in rust by eating through the metal surfaces.

Rust Prevention

Due to the importance and widespread use of steel and iron and its products, prevention of rust is of very high importance and several specialized methods were developed to come up with ways to stop it. A short overview of the methods is discussed here.

Rust is known to be permeable to water and air, and the interior iron located beneath a layer of rust continue to corrode. Prevention then requires a coating to prevent the formation of rust.

Alloys that are rust-resistant

Special alloys rust somewhat slower since the rust clings to the metal's surface in a protected layer. Designs that use this material are required to include measures to avoid the worst exposures, as it will still continue to slowly rust under even almost ideal conditions.

Galvanization

Galvanization occurs when zinc is applied by either electroplating or hot-dipping. Zinc is used most of the time since it is not expensive, clings to the steel well, and adds protection to the surface of the steel in case there is damage to the zinc.

In a more corrosive environment, similar to that of salt water, cadmium is a better option. It both instances, this coating provides partial protection to the cathode by working as a galvanic anode and thereby corroding itself rather than the protected underlying metal. The zinc is consumed and the galvanization then provides protection for a limited time period.

Modern coatings have added aluminium known as zinc-alume; the aluminium will move to conceal scratches and then provides protection longer. This approach relies on the aluminium and zinc oxides to protect a surface that is scratched, other than a sacrificial anode as used in conventional galvanized coatings. Sometimes, both a coating and zinc are used to enhance the corrosion protection.

Cathodic protection

Cathodic protection consists of a technique that is used for slowing the corrosion process on immersed or buried structures by providing an electrical charge which overpowers the electrochemical reaction. When applied correctly, the corrosion can be completely avoided. In its simplest formula, it can be attained by attaching a sacrificial anode, and thereby making the steel or iron the cathode.

This sacrificial anode has to be made from something that has a more negative electrode potential, commonly zinc, aluminium, or magnesium. The sacrificial anode eventually will corrode, ending its protective action replaced in a timely manner.

Cathodic protection is also provided with a special electrical device that appropriately induces an electric charge.

Painting and coatings

Formation of rust can be prevented using such coatings as varnish, paint, and lacquer which protects the iron from its environment. Automobiles and ships are examples of large structures that have box sections enclosed and have products that are wax-based injected into these sections for protection. These treatments will also usually contain rust inhibitors. Covering of steel with concreate can add some protection because of its alkaline pH environment. However, there can still be a rust problem since the expanding rust can fracture the concrete.

When short-term protection is required for transport or storage, you can add a thin layer of grease, oil, or Cosmoline to the surface of the iron. These treatments are used extensively when storing an automobile, steel ship, or other item for a long period of time.

There are antisieze mixtures available for application to metallic threads and other machined surfaces to protect them against rust. They usually consist of grease mixed with zinc, aluminium powder, or copper, and other exclusive ingredients.

Bluing

This consists of a technique that provides limited resistance for smaller steel items to rusting, including firearms. However, in order for it work, an oil that displaces water must be rubbed on the blue steel and the other steel.

Inhibitors

Gas-phase and volatile inhibitors, known as corrosion inhibitors, are used in prevention of corrosion inside a sealed system. These will not work out side of a sealed system as the circulation of air will disperse them and bring in moisture and oxygen.

Humidity

By controlling the moisture, rust can be prevented. The silica gel packets are used to control the humidity that might occur when something is shipped by sea.

Removal of Rust

Rust removal can be done at home using a procedure known as electrolysis. This requires a plastic bucket, rebar, tap water, bailing wire, washing soda, and a battery charger.

Rust can also be treated with some commercial products containing tannic acid, which will combine with the rust. These products are known as rust converters.

Economic effect

The degradation of iron-based structures and tools is associated with rust. Since it has a higher volume that its originating mass, this buildup also causes failure in forcing adjacent parts to separate, which is also called "rust packing". This caused the fall of the Mianus bridge in 1983, when its bearings internally rusted and pushed a corner of the road slab from its support.

OPEN
SHUT

It was also a vital factor involved in the 1967 Silver Bridge disaster in West Virginia. In less than a minute a steel suspension bridge fell and killed 46 people on the bridge. In Pennsylvania, the Kinzua Bridge was blown down in 2003 by a tornado, largely due to the fact that the base bolts had rusted, leaving the bridge anchored only by gravity.

Reinforced concrete can also be susceptible to rust damage. The internal pressure caused by the expanding corrosion of steel and iron covered by concrete can cause it to spall, creating significant structural problems. It is one of the more common failures of reinforced concrete buildings and bridges.

For more information about metals rust, research the internet, go to your local library, and ask questions of your teachers, family, and friends.

Visit

BABY PROFESSOR
EDUCATION KIDS

www.BabyProfessorBooks.com
to download Free Baby Professor eBooks
and view our catalog of new and exciting
Children's Books